IT'S TIME TO EAT GARLIC TOAST

It's Time to Eat GARLIC TOAST

Walter the Educator

Silent King Books
A WhichHead Entertainment Imprint

Copyright © 2024 by Walter the Educator

All rights reserved. No part of this book may be reproduced in any manner whatsoever without written per- mission except in the case of brief quotations embodied in critical articles and reviews.

First Printing, 2024

Disclaimer

This book is a literary work; the story is not about specific persons, locations, situations, and/or circumstances unless mentioned in a historical context. Any resemblance to real persons, locations, situations, and/or circumstances is coincidental. This book is for entertainment and informational purposes only. The author and publisher offer this information without warranties expressed or implied. No matter the grounds, neither the author nor the publisher will be accountable for any losses, injuries, or other damages caused by the reader's use of this book. The use of this book acknowledges an understanding and acceptance of this disclaimer.

It's Time to Eat GARLIC TOAST is a collectible early learning book by Walter the Educator suitable for all ages belonging to Walter the Educator's Time to Eat Book Series. Collect more books at WaltertheEducator.com

USE THE EXTRA SPACE TO TAKE NOTES AND DOCUMENT YOUR MEMORIES

GARLIC TOAST

Golden slices, warm and bright,

It's Time to Eat

Garlic Toast

Garlic toast is such a delight!

Crunchy edges, soft inside,

A tasty treat we just can't hide.

Butter spreads in a creamy way,

With garlic sprinkles to make our day.

Herbs like parsley, green and neat,

Add a sparkle to our treat.

Into the oven, it starts to bake,

The kitchen smells so good, we ache!

The toast turns brown with a gentle glow,

It's almost ready, just watch it show.

Out it comes, so warm and hot,

A plate of goodness, we've got a lot!

Each slice is perfect, crisp and light,

It's time to eat, what a delight!

It's Time to Eat

Garlic Toast

Dip it in soup, or eat it plain,

Garlic toast is never mundane.

A crunchy sound with every bite,

It's garlicky fun, pure delight.

Share it with family, pass it around,

The joy of garlic toast always astounds.

Big slices, small slices, all the same,

Each one is part of the garlic toast game.

Pair it with pasta, twirly and long,

Garlic toast makes every meal strong.

A bite of toast, a sip of tea,

It's the perfect combo, you'll agree!

Sprinkle some cheese for a melty surprise,

Watch it stretch as it meets our eyes.

Garlic toast, oh what a dish,

It's Time to Eat

Garlic

Toast

Every slice fulfills a wish.

So grab your fork or use your hands,

Garlic toast love forever stands.

A simple treat, but the very best,

Garlic toast beats all the rest!

Morning or evening, it's always the same,

Garlic toast shines in the flavor game.

A bite of joy, both crispy and neat,

It's Time to Eat Garlic Toast

Garlic toast time is the best to eat!

ABOUT THE CREATOR

Walter the Educator is one of the pseudonyms for Walter Anderson. Formally educated in Chemistry, Business, and Education, he is an educator, an author, a diverse entrepreneur, and he is the son of a disabled war veteran. "Walter the Educator" shares his time between educating and creating. He holds interests and owns several creative projects that entertain, enlighten, enhance, and educate, hoping to inspire and motivate you. Follow, find new works, and stay up to date with Walter the Educator™ at WaltertheEducator.com

www.ingramcontent.com/pod-product-compliance
Lightning Source LLC
LaVergne TN
LVHW012052070526
838201LV00082B/3987